W9-BXX-306

Martin Luther King Jr.

Fulfilling a Dream

Jacqueline Conciatore Senter

New York

Published in 2018 by Cavendish Square Publishing, LLC
243 5th Avenue, Suite 136, New York, NY 10016

Copyright © 2018 by Cavendish Square Publishing, LLC

First Edition

No part of this publication may be reproduced, stored in a retrieval system, or transmitted in any form or by any means—electronic, mechanical, photocopying, recording, or otherwise—without the prior permission of the copyright owner. Request for permission should be addressed to Permissions, Cavendish Square Publishing, 243 5th Avenue, Suite 136, New York, NY 10016. Tel (877) 980-4450; fax (877) 980-4454.

Website: cavendishsq.com

This publication represents the opinions and views of the author based on his or her personal experience, knowledge, and research. The information in this book serves as a general guide only. The author and publisher have used their best efforts in preparing this book and disclaim liability rising directly or indirectly from the use and application of this book.

All websites were available and accurate when this book was sent to press.

Library of Congress Cataloging-in-Publication Data

Names: Senter, Jacqueline Conciatore, author.
Title: Martin Luther King Jr. : fulfilling a dream / Jacqueline Conciatore Senter.
Description: New York : Cavendish Square Publishing, [2018] | Series: Peaceful protesters | Includes bibliographical references and index.
Identifiers: LCCN 2017019399 (print) | LCCN 2017019735 (ebook) | ISBN 9781502631169 (library bound) | ISBN 9781502633958 (Paperback) | ISBN 9781502631176 (E-book)
Subjects: LCSH: King, Martin Luther, Jr., 1929-1968--Juvenile literature. | African Americans--Biography--Juvenile literature. | Civil rights workers--United States--Biography--Juvenile literature. | African Americans--Civil rights--History--20th century--Juvenile literature. | Civil rights movements--United States--History--20th century--Juvenile literature.
Classification: LCC E185.97.K5 (ebook) | LCC E185.97.K5 S47 2018 (print) | DDC 323.092 [B] --dc23
LC record available at https://lccn.loc.gov/2017019399

Editorial Director: David McNamara
Editor: Caitlyn Miller
Copy Editor: Nathan Heidelberger
Associate Art Director: Amy Greenan
Designer: Alan Sliwinski
Production Coordinator: Karol Szymczuk
Photo Research: J8 Media

The photographs in this book are used by permission and through the courtesy of: Cover, p. 1 Howard Sochurek/The LIFE Picture Collection/Getty Images; Background image used throughout ilolab/Shutterstock.com; p. 4 AP Photo/Gene Herrick; p. 16 Stephen F. Somerstein/Getty Images; p. 18 Afro American Newspapers/Gado/Getty Images; p. 21 Bettmann/Getty Images; p. 24 Currier and Ives/File:First Colored Senator and Representatives.jpg/Wikimedia Commons; p. 29 Jack Delano/File:WhiteDoorColoredDoor.jpg/Wikimedia Commons; p. 30 Russell Lee/File:"Colored" drinking fountain from mid-20th century with african-american drinking.jpg/Wikimedia Commons; p. 35 Unknown/File:The color line still exists—in this case cph.3b29638.jpg/Wikimedia Commons; p. 42 Don Cravens/The LIFE Images Collection/Getty Images; p. 43 City of Birmingham, Alabama/File:Bull Connor (1960).jpg/Wikimedia Commons; p. 45 NY Daily News Archive via Getty Images; p. 46 Unknown/File:Mohandas K. Gandhi, portrait.jpg/Wikimedia Commons; p. 51 AP Photo/Chuck Burton; p. 53 Bettmann/Getty Images; p. 57 Lee Lockwood/The LIFE Images Collection/Getty Images; p. 58 Bettmann/Getty Images; p. 60 AP Photo/Horace Cort; p. 66 Bettmann/Getty Images; p. 69 Michael Ochs Archives/Getty Images; p. 75 AP Photo; p. 76 Bob Parent/Getty Images; p. 79 Rolls Press/Popperfoto/Getty Images; p. 81 Universal History Archive/Getty Images; p. 85 Bettmann/Getty Images; p. 88 Popperfoto/Getty Images; p. 90 Hulton Archive/Getty Images; p. 94 Joseph Louw/The LIFE Images Collection/Getty Images; p. 96 National Geographic Creative/Alamy Stock Photo.

Printed in the United States of America

CONTENTS

A young Martin Luther King at the pulpit of Holt Street Baptist Church, a rallying point during the Montgomery bus boycott

CHAPTER ONE

Who Was Martin Luther King Jr.?

On Monday, December 5, 1955, the African American citizens of Montgomery, Alabama, faced an important decision. Thousands of people gathered at the Holt Street Baptist Church to discuss and weigh their options. In fact, so many people gathered that the church overflowed; most participants were forced to remain outside on the street, listening to the evening's proceedings as they were broadcast over loudspeakers.

The answer to the question at hand that evening would change history: Should they collectively refuse to ride Montgomery's buses, standing united against the injustice of **segregation**? The Southern system of segregation—known colloquially as **Jim Crow**—separated African Americans from white people just about everywhere: restaurants, waiting rooms, hospitals, and more. The Jim Crow laws, among other restrictions, forced black people to sit at the back of buses and to give up seats to white people when the front filled up.

Fighting segregation was always dangerous. A boycott of the city buses could have devastating consequences for the African Americans of Montgomery, who would now be activists, fighting for justice with their feet and their wallets. Those who participated in the boycott knew they might lose their jobs, be spit at on the street, or be arrested. Far worse, they were risking their lives.

Among the throngs of people at the church, a few attendees stood out from the crowd. One such figure was Rosa Parks. Four days earlier, she had refused to give her bus seat to a white man. Parks had been arrested, and her case had sparked a one-day bus boycott on that very day (December 5). Thousands of black workers stayed home, walked, or found other rides to work, and the city buses rolled along, empty.

Also in attendance was the new pastor of the Dexter Avenue Baptist Church. His youthful looks belied his power. His voice was deep and sonorous, reverberating around the church, as he spoke from the heart:

"

You know, my friends, there comes a time when people get tired of being trampled over by the iron feet of oppression … We are here, we are here this evening, because we're tired now … Right here in Montgomery, when the history books are written in the future, somebody will have to say, "There lived a race of people, a black people, 'fleecy locks and black complexion,' a people who had the moral courage to stand up for their rights. And thereby they injected a new meaning into the veins of history and of civilization!"

For a few moments, the people were quiet, but then they cheered, and clapped, and clapped some more. Their applause was like thunder. Ultimately, they voted to continue the **Montgomery bus boycott** for however long it would take to end segregation on Montgomery's buses. They knew the risks; and they knew, too, that Dr. Martin Luther King Jr. had arrived.

A Happy Early Life

Martin Luther King Jr. was born on January 15, 1929, in a handsome two-story clapboard house on Auburn Avenue in Atlanta, the capital city of Georgia. Martin's given name at birth was actually Michael, and the family called him "Little Mike." Martin's father, also named Michael, changed their names in honor of Martin Luther, a sixteenth-century religious reformer and founder of the Lutheran Church.

Auburn Avenue was known as a center of African American prosperity, with middle-class homes on one end and black-owned businesses on the other. Thus, it had a nickname: "Sweet Auburn." Martin's early life was sweet, too—happy, comfortable, and full of love. His home was lively and intergenerational, with his father, mother, sister, brother, mother's parents, and aunt all under one roof. The house was usually bustling with guests and church visitors.

Daily routines made for strong family bonds. Martin's father insisted they all sit down for dinner every night, no matter how late he came home from work. The children had to recite a Bible verse before eating, and often Martin and his younger brother, A. D., chose the Good Book's shortest verse: "Jesus wept." The King family's discussions around the table ranged from what was happening in the community, to school, to politics. Martin, A. D., and their older sister, Willie, were encouraged to join the conversation. Often, after dinner, the family moved into the parlor and played games. Martin's favorite game was Monopoly, which he often won. The parlor served as a music room as well. Martin's mother, Alberta, was a classically trained singer, and Martin had a beautiful voice. The family sang church hymns around the piano and listened to gospel records and other music on the Victrola.

Although he would grow up to be the world's most famous **civil rights** leader, and an inspiration to millions, Martin had a typical childhood. He liked shooting hoops with the neighborhood firefighters, loved baseball, and was an avid reader. He also had a mischievous streak. Once, he hid in a bush along the walkway, holding a stick attached to one of his mother's fox-fur stoles. When people passed by, he startled them, poking the stick out of the bush. Another time, he and A. D. loosened the legs of a piano stool so that when their poor music teacher sat, she crashed to the floor. The boys thought it was hilarious, but their father did not, whipping them as punishment.

As early as the age of six, Martin was aware of people less fortunate. In 1935, because of the Great Depression, many Americans were jobless, scraping by with little money, even going hungry. Riding in the car with his parents one day, Martin saw a crowd of people waiting on a sidewalk. It was a breadline, his parents explained, and the people were there to receive free food. The memory of this scene stayed with Martin into adulthood.

As Good as Anyone

Life for African American people in the American South was constantly tense—at its best. At its worst, it was cruel and unjust. The reality for African Americans was that they could be beaten, jailed, or even killed if they angered a white person.

Even for a child sheltered by a loving family, growing up in this world wasn't easy. In his father, however, Martin had a strong role model. Martin Luther King Sr. was a large man who stood tall and did *not* bow to other men. One day, Martin and his father went into a shoe store and sat in the first row of seats, waiting to try on shoes. A white clerk walked over to them and, in a low voice, asked them to switch to seats farther back. Martin's father said, "There's nothing wrong with these seats ... We'll either buy shoes sitting here, or we won't buy shoes at all." He took Martin's hand and they left.

In another incident, which Martin wrote about as an adult, his father drove through a stop sign:

> "
>
> *A policeman pulled up to the car and said, "All right, boy, pull over and let me see your license." My father instantly retorted: "Let me make it clear to you that you aren't talking to a boy. If you persist in referring to me as a boy, I will be forced to act as if I don't hear a word you are saying." The policeman was so shocked ... he nervously wrote the ticket and left the scene as quickly as possible.*

Martin's mother showed the same kind of fortitude as his father, though she was not intimidating like Martin Sr. She "instilled a sense of self-respect in all of her children from the very beginning," Martin said. She explained segregation, racism, and white hatred to her children. She talked about slavery and the Civil War. She told her children that segregation was a man-made thing, not natural at all. And she told her children they should fight for their rights. "Then," said Martin, "she said the words that almost every Negro hears before he can yet understand the injustice that makes them necessary: 'You are as good as anyone.'"

Hatred and Beyond

Back then, a black child in the South was certain to witness and feel the terrible injustice of Jim Crow and racism. When Martin was about eight, in a downtown Atlanta store with his mother, a white lady slapped him. Using a racial epithet, she accused him of having stepped on her foot. By the time Martin told Alberta what had happened, the woman was gone.

Several years later, returning home by bus from a speech contest he'd won, Martin and his teacher were told to give their seats to white passengers. Martin wanted to stay seated, but his teacher urged him to get up. The teen who had just won first prize for his speech, "The Negro and the Constitution," stood in the aisle with his teacher for 90 miles (145 kilometers). "It was the angriest I have ever been in my life," Martin would say later.

The summer before college, Martin traveled to Simsbury, Connecticut, to earn money picking tobacco. The group of boys he traveled with chose him to be their prayer leader, and he enjoyed the new role. Although busy, he wrote letters to his parents from Simsbury. His letters reveal how surprised Martin was to be treated differently in the North, which did not have Jim Crow. "After we passed Washington there was no discrimination at all. The white people here are very nice. We go to any place we want to and sit anywhere we want to."

But of course, this new way of life was temporary. On the train returning to the South, Martin had to move to a segregated car. "The first time I was seated behind a curtain in a dining car, I felt as if the curtain had been dropped on my selfhood," he wrote.

"

I could never adjust to the separate waiting rooms, separate eating places, separate rest rooms, partly because the separate was always unequal, and partly because the very idea of separation did something to my sense of dignity and self-respect.

Through these myriad experiences of racism, Martin developed a hatred of white people as a young man.

However, when he entered Morehouse College, he joined student groups that were fighting racism and injustice. There were black *and* white students in these groups, and he saw that he could safely view at least some white people as allies—especially young white people. He nurtured a "spirit of cooperation" in his heart, where there had been resentment before.

"A Flame That Would Shoot Across America"

Refusing to hate is a theme of Martin Luther King Jr.'s adult life. He was, after all, raised in the Christian faith. His family's Baptist church practiced the **social gospel**. This meant using Jesus Christ's teachings—such as "Love thy neighbor"—to consider and attack social problems, including racial injustice. It meant thinking about how things were going here on earth, as well as how they might be one day in heaven. Martin's father and maternal grandfather, both preachers, did not focus only on spiritual questions of sin or salvation. Their ministries were political, too. Martin's father had led a campaign to raise black teacher salaries so they equaled white teacher salaries. Martin's grandfather had been president of the Atlanta chapter of the **NAACP,** one of the country's leading groups fighting for equality. He also had led a boycott against a local newspaper that disparaged blacks.

Martin entered Morehouse College in 1944, at age fifteen. (He'd skipped the ninth and twelfth grades.) While a freshman, he read an essay that would influence his own philosophy and goals: **Henry David Thoreau**'s "**Civil Disobedience**." Thoreau was a nineteenth-century thinker, writer, and abolitionist. He refused to pay taxes as a protest against slavery and the Mexican-American War, which he regarded as an act of international aggression by the United States. Like many abolitionists, Thoreau believed the war would lead to new slave territories. Indeed, Southern planters—those who ran slave plantations—admitted they wanted to expand westward. In "Civil Disobedience," Thoreau told people to refuse to cooperate with a government that sanctioned slavery and conquered another country to take its land.

Reading the essay, King said he was "fascinated by the idea of refusing to cooperate with an evil system," and was so "deeply moved that [he] reread the work several times." He became convinced, he wrote, that not cooperating with evil systems—like segregation—was as important as participating in just systems.

King wanted to be a lawyer, to take the fight against Jim Crow to the courts. His father and grandfather had made noble examples for him, but Martin resisted the idea of being a preacher. For one thing, he doubted the truth of certain Bible stories. Even at the age of thirteen, he'd questioned how Jesus's body could have risen from the dead. Also, he worried that religion could not be squared with scientific fact and wondered whether it could be "intellectually respectable as well as emotionally satisfying."

But at Morehouse, he learned another way to read the Bible, looking for the deep truths behind such stories as Adam and Eve in the Garden of Eden or Jonah being swallowed by a whale. He also met ministers who were not only intellectuals but respected educators making a real difference in the world. "I could see in their lives the ideal of what I wanted a minister to be," he said. King always recognized in himself a strong urge to serve humanity. Now he recognized the desire to become a preacher.

After graduating from Morehouse, King studied at Crozer Seminary in Pennsylvania and then Boston University. During these years, he took up questions about human nature, evil in society, and social justice. He came to know the life and ideas of **Mahatma Gandhi**, who had led India's people in a nonviolent revolt against British rule. (Gandhi died in 1948, the same year King graduated from Morehouse and started at Crozer.) While Americans had won independence from Britain in a war, Gandhi helped free his people from the British peacefully. King began to think about the possibilities for using **nonviolent resistance** in the South. He became personally committed to the principles of nonviolence. Black people had to fight for equality, he believed, but they had to do it peacefully.

Going Home to Make a Difference

Dr. King and Coretta Scott King were married in 1953.

In Boston, Martin met a smart, attractive, Southern woman who was studying classical music. Coretta Scott wasn't sure about Martin at first. She wasn't used to preachers and didn't know much about them, but it didn't take long before Coretta, whom King called Corrie, fell for Martin.

They were married in her parents' garden on June 18, 1953. Although life was better for them in the North, they decided to move back to the South because it was their home. When a Montgomery, Alabama, church offered Martin a position as pastor, he and Coretta decided they didn't want to be "detached spectators" to the struggles of blacks in the Deep South. They wanted to be part of history and to help.

King would bring his desire to serve, rejection of hatred, and, perhaps most importantly, his commitment to nonviolent **direct action** to Montgomery. His rousing speech on December 5, 1955, was one of many, many speeches that would stir people to action and bring out their hope, determination, and even forgiveness for white people's actions. That night in December, a reporter described King and this burgeoning movement as the beginning of "a flame that would go across America."

From here, our story will trace that flame. We'll see how Dr. King and many other courageous people—ordinary people—fought segregation. We will be shaken by tragedies such as the murder of Emmett Till, a fourteen-year-old boy who was targeted due to the color of skin, nothing more. We'll be inspired by the bravery of activists who risked their lives to simply sit at lunch counters or use rest facilities at bus stops. We'll see Dr. King lead people as they are beaten, jailed, and even killed—and still fight on peacefully. We'll see that during these events King himself was both praised and, probably more often, pummeled. He traveled from protest marches on dusty Alabama streets to the smooth corridors of the White House, from jail cells to a podium in Norway to accept the Nobel Peace Prize, and back again to jail. We'll also stop in Washington, DC, where, on the Lincoln Memorial's marble steps, the Reverend Dr. Martin Luther King Jr. gave one of the most powerful and memorable speeches ever given.

We'll also head back to Montgomery, where people will soon have weary and aching feet. The bus boycott will last longer than they ever imagined it would: 381 days.

Mamie Till Bradley changed history by insisting her son's casket be open, to show what had been done to Emmett.

CHAPTER TWO

The Struggle for Integration and Voting Rights

A few months before that historic meeting at the Holt Street Church, attention in the black community and beyond turned to Mississippi, where a brutal, heartless murder revealed the magnitude of injustice in the land of Jim Crow. In August 1955, two white men (possibly more) killed fourteen-year-old Emmett Till, an outgoing boy who loved to joke around and play pranks and had his whole life ahead of him. The killing was a lynching—a type of murder committed by more than one person and often a mob of people. Radical **segregationists** in the South used lynchings to inspire fear in African Americans—in other words, as a form of terrorism. The men involved here, Roy Bryant and J. W. Milam, beat up and shot Till, tied a cotton-gin fan around his dead body, and threw Till's body into a river, believing that Till had flirted with Bryant's wife.

Till was from Chicago and unaccustomed to the South's strict—in fact, life or death— codes of conduct. Some witnesses said Till "wolf whistled" at Carolyn Bryant in the grocery store she owned with her husband; others said he walked past her and said, "Bye, Baby." During the murder trial, Bryant would say Till had grabbed her hand and waist and spoken suggestively. However, decades later Bryant confessed she had lied to help her husband avoid a guilty charge. Till hadn't been menacing, she said, adding, "Nothing that boy did could ever justify what happened to him."

Bryant's testimony probably made no difference, as the all-white, male jury wanted to acquit. The jury deliberated for one hour—and only that long to "make it look good," one jury member said. Months later, in an interview for *Look* magazine, Bryant and Milam described how they killed Till. They felt free to admit their guilt because of the law—no citizen in the United States can be tried twice for the same charges with the same facts, once acquitted.

In Chicago, Till's mother, Mamie Till Bradley, insisted the casket be open during her son's memorial service.

"I wanted the world to see what they did to my baby," she said. She could not know that this act, having people look upon Emmett Till's destroyed face and body, would help spur the civil rights movement to a new level. Thousands came to the service and walked by the casket, and thousands more saw photos in newspapers. The world was now more aware of the terrible injustice in the American South.

King would speak often to crowds of Emmett Till, and he said the murder "might be considered one of the most brutal and inhuman crimes of the twentieth century." Till's death could not have been far from people's minds in Montgomery three months later, when they voted to continue the bus boycott.

Tens of thousands of mourners attended fourteen-year-old Emmett Till's funeral in Chicago.

Reconstruction

It could be said that the kind of systemic racism that allowed Emmett Till's murderers to walk free was actually decades in the making. After the Civil War ended in 1865, four million slaves were suddenly free, and the Union had been preserved. But many parts of the South were in ruins. Cities, towns, and homes were destroyed, and some people were starving. Hundreds of thousands of men and boys were dead, many others were maimed, and, without slave labor, the South could not restore its plantation economy.

While the job of rebuilding the South would be massive, people with various motives—charitable, industrious, and opportunistic—rose to the challenge. Northern missionaries traveled South to start schools for freed black children. Men of business, derisively called "carpetbaggers" by Southerners who saw them as greedy intruders, sought opportunities to make a profit and perhaps build something new. The Freedmen's Bureau (Bureau of Refugees, Freedmen, and Abandoned Lands), which Congress established before the war even ended, ensured freed people and poor whites had food, shelter, jobs, health care, and education.

This period of **Reconstruction** (1865–1877) would see progress made for freed people and then much of that progress reversed. One important player was the new president, Andrew Johnson, who had been vice president before Abraham Lincoln was killed. Some Northerners wanted Johnson to punish the wealthy plantation owners who led the Confederate rebellion. But Johnson, a Southerner and former slaveholder himself, was lenient. Former Confederates pledged loyalty to the Union and asked him for a pardon, and Johnson gave them back their lands. As someone born into poverty who'd been a tailor before embarking on a political career, he enjoyed the sight of elite people humbled before him. Soon, many of the same white men who had been influential before the Civil War were back in positions of state and local authority. These men, Southern Democrats, established laws called "Black Codes" that limited the activities of freed people. A few Black Codes gave freed people new rights, such as the right to own property. But most were oppressive. They made it illegal for black citizens to do things like bear arms, read or write, or own or lease land. Many of the codes were designed to force freed blacks to return to the plantations and plantation homes to work. Seeing this, Northerners were incensed. Why had they fought a war, losing more than 360,000 men and boys, only to have the South revert to slavery in all but name?

A group of Washington, DC, politicians known as the Radical Republicans stepped in. They helped push through Congress a law designed to protect the rights of freed peoples: the Civil Rights Act of 1866. They also helped pass the Fourteenth Amendment, which granted citizenship to blacks and required states to guarantee equal protection under the law. Finally, Congress, under the influence of the Radical Republicans, sent federal troops to the South to ensure the new rights were upheld.

The new arrangement improved many aspects of life for black people. Many registered to vote, and in some cities and states, African Americans were elected into office, including as members of Congress. In fact, sixteen African Americans served as members of Congress during Reconstruction.

But about ten years later, as part of political deal-making that had guaranteed him the White House, President Rutherford B. Hayes pulled the federal troops

The seven Southern men depicted in this Currier and Ives print were the first African Americans elected to Congress.

out of the South. Democrats who'd been sidelined during the Northern occupation now had a clear path to take over. They quickly set about reversing the progress African Americans had made under Reconstruction. People were now even freer to use intimidation and violence to keep blacks from exercising their right to vote. **Vigilante** groups could roam the countryside at night, terrorizing black families.

Reconstruction had made some permanent progress, though. Around 20 percent of African Americans in the South had acquired land by 1880, according to scholars at the University of Houston. The first state-run schools and hospitals for African Americans had been established, as well as the first black colleges and independent black churches. However, the era of hopeful change for the South was over; Jim Crow was just ahead.

A Closer Look at Jim Crow

No one knows for sure how the term "Jim Crow" originated. In the 1800s, a white stage performer named Thomas "Daddy" Rice helped popularize the phrase. He was one of the first minstrel showmen, meaning his performances featured clownish, offensive stereotypes that were supposed to be amusing. He played a poor, lame black man who danced and sang:

“

Weel a-bout and turn a-bout
And do just so.
Every time I weel a-bout
I jump Jim Crow.

Others say the character Jim Crow goes back much further, to African folklore, where he is an actual crow and a trickster. Whatever the origins of the name, it has become a widely understood reference to the segregation laws and conditions of the South from the end of the nineteenth century until the middle of the twentieth century.

Separate but Equal

A less mysterious name to know when talking about segregation and racism in the South is Plessy. Homer Plessy was an educated man of mixed race. In 1892, he entered a whites-only Louisiana train car as a challenge to the state's "separate but equal" policy, which said that segregation was acceptable as long as equal facilities were provided to African Americans. Plessy was arrested and convicted. The case went through appeals all the way to the United States Supreme Court. In a ruling many people regard as one of the court's worst (along with the 1857 Dred Scott decision, which said that African

Americans were not citizens), the justices ruled 7–1 that "separate but equal" did not violate the Constitution. If the train cars for blacks were equal, segregation was constitutional, the court said. This decision allowed the continuation and the spread of Jim Crow.

"The Supreme Court of this nation through the *Plessy v. Ferguson* decision, established the doctrine of separate but equal as the law of the land," said King in a 1956 speech. "But we all know what happened as a result of that doctrine; there was always a strict enforcement of the separate without the slightest intention to abide by the equal."

In this same speech, King talked about how he had recently been part of a group being seated for lunch in an Atlanta airport restaurant. The all-white group (except for King) was escorted into the main dining room, while King was escorted into a back room. He confronted the restaurant manager, who said his establishment had to obey state segregation laws and city ordinances. But, the manager insisted, King would get the same service and the same food, even on the same dishes:

"

And I looked at him and started wondering if he really believed that. And I started talking with him. I said, "Now, I don't see how I can get the same service. Number one, I confront aesthetic inequality. I can't see all these beautiful pictures that you have around the walls here. We don't have them back there. But not only that, I just don't like sitting back there and it does something to me. It makes me almost angry. I know that I shouldn't get angry. I know that I shouldn't become bitter, but when you put me back there something happens to my soul, so that I confront inequality in the sense that I have a greater potential for the accumulation of bitterness because you put me back there."

King was being somewhat humorous in that speech, but there was seriousness there, too. Segregation measures in the South were *everywhere*—a continual affront to the spirit. Buses, taxis, trains, restaurants, movie theaters, restrooms, drinking fountains, pools, and schools—all were segregated. Even churches and public libraries were segregated. Like backyard weeds, signs marked spaces with labels such as "Colored Waiting Room," "White Only," "Colored Seated in Rear," and "Colored Entrance."

States went to great lengths to ensure separation of the races. In the courtroom, whites and blacks had to swear on separate Bibles. In some states, textbooks couldn't be shared between white and "colored" schools. In one South Carolina cotton mill, according to author Juan Williams in *Eyes on the Prize*, black workers weren't allowed to look out of the same window as white workers. Many Jim Crow laws revealed the fear whites had of living in a society that embraced integration. Many whites especially feared interracial marriage. In Mississippi, for example, anyone who distributed written material in favor of social equality or intermarriage was subject to a fine of up to $500, six months in jail, or both.

It's important to note that although the South practiced blatant racism and created laws to support racist ideas, there was also discrimination and racism in other parts of the country. In the Northern states, blacks and whites might have ridden the same buses, but they generally lived in different neighborhoods and looked askance at interracial marriages. Northern whites discriminated against blacks in hiring, selling or renting housing, social situations, and other everyday scenarios. Some people argued that

This 1940 photograph shows separate entrances for whites and blacks into a Durham, North Carolina, café.

In the Jim Crow South, segregation was everywhere—even at drinking fountains like this one in Oklahoma City, Oklahoma, in 1939.

Northern whites favored racial equality as a *concept*—in the abstract. But Northerners, they argued, were intolerant toward black people individually. Southern whites, on the other hand, sometimes had close personal relationships with blacks, who often worked in their homes, but were intolerant in the abstract.

Brown v. Board of Education

Jim Crow hurt black children in several ways. Black schools in the South were overcrowded and in poor condition. Sometimes, schools for black students were little more than tar-paper shacks. Jim Crow states spent far more per white child than they did per black child. In the late 1940s, a group of researchers studied the effects of this inequality. Here's some of what they found, recounted in *Jim Crow's Children* by Peter Irons:

“

Behind the school is a small building with a broken, sagging door. As we approach, a nervous, middle-aged woman comes to the door of the school. She greets us in a discouraged voice marked by a speech impediment. Escorted inside, we observe that the broken benches are crowded to three times their normal capacity. Only a few battered books are in sight, and we look in vain for maps or charts. We learn that four grades are assembled here. The weary teacher agrees to permit us to remain while she proceeds with the instruction. She goes to the blackboard and writes an assignment for the first two grades to do while she conducts spelling and word drills for the third and fourth grades.

NAACP lawyers worked for years to bring about an end to segregation, including school segregation, through the courts. In 1953, the Supreme Court took up the issue in a case called ***Brown v. Board of Education***. *Brown* actually combined five cases, all dealing with school segregation. The NAACP argued that segregated schools were unequal and that segregation harmed the spirits of black children. On May 17, 1954, the court unanimously held that segregation in schools was unconstitutional and detrimental to children. “Separate educational facilities are inherently unequal," the decision stated. The court had overturned the decision made in *Plessy v. Ferguson*.

This was the new law of the land, but still Southern states resisted desegregation. In fact, the first black students to enter a white high school, in Little Rock, Arkansas, met such rage from segregationists that President Dwight Eisenhower had to send in federal troops: the 101st Airborne Division of the US Army. These soldiers had to accompany the nine students inside Central High School. White students abused the "Little Rock Nine" students throughout their time at the formerly all-white high school, but eight of the nine students endured through graduation.

In the rural Prince William County, Virginia, officials closed the public schools for five years rather than integrate. In the United States Congress, Southern lawmakers wrote and signed a "Declaration of Constitutional Principles," later known as the "Southern Manifesto," that accused the Supreme Court of abusing its power with the *Brown* decision. They encouraged states to resist integration. The Supreme Court would make additional rulings to back up *Brown* and get states to finally integrate schools.

For reasons that should now be clear, *Brown v. Board* was only the beginning of the modern civil rights era. There would be battles ahead over segregation, as well as for voting rights.

Citizens' Councils and the KKK

White Citizens' Councils sprung up throughout the South after *Brown*. These councils included leading men in the community like business owners and politicians, as well as others such as bus drivers. When African Americans tried to vote, fight segregation, or demand other rights, the councils practiced something called "economic reprisal." They'd arrange for the person's job to be threatened, or for that person to be fired; perhaps the aspiring voter would be evicted. Other tactics the councils used included boycotting black-owned businesses, denying loans to blacks, and calling in loans for full payment even if the loan was in good standing. During the Montgomery bus boycott, the city's mayor joined the Citizens' Council and urged all Montgomery whites to do the same.

Another tactic, like in the case of Emmett Till, was vigilante reprisals. These reprisals included cross burnings, beatings, lynchings, and home bombings. These kinds of attacks are generally associated with the Ku Klux Klan (KKK), a white terrorist group in the South. Nearly 4,500 African Americans were lynched in the United States between 1882 and the early 1950s. Medgar Evers, the NAACP chair in Jackson, Mississippi, was killed by a member of the local Citizens' Council on the same day that President John F. Kennedy gave a televised speech calling for national civil rights legislation.

Voting Rights

Blacks in the South believed that if they could vote freely, they would be able to elect politicians who'd look out for their interests. Elected black officials could be a foil to the Citizens' Councils. And once blacks could vote, they could serve on juries, which would be a step toward seeking justice against vigilantes. But these were exactly the outcomes white segregationists didn't want.

The Fifteenth Amendment gave black men the legal right to vote in 1870 (women did not yet have the right), during Reconstruction. Blacks faced fewer barriers to voting in this period, but there was never a time when white segregationists didn't try to keep blacks from the ballot box. In 1873, for example, whites in Colfax, Louisiana, killed scores of freedmen—perhaps as many as 150—during a contested gubernatorial election.

Black voting in the South dwindled in the face of these harsh realities. The Democratic Party, which favored segregation, won all the elections. It solidified its control of the South. In fact, the Southern states became known as the "Solid South" because they were an unbroken block of majority white Democrats.

Black **suffrage**, or the right to vote, would take another hit toward the end of the nineteenth century, when Mississippi decided its citizens had to pass a **literacy test** to vote. To successfully register as voters, Mississippians

This 1879 *Harper's Weekly* cartoon shows a man called "Mr. Solid South" justifying literacy tests at the voting booth.

had to prove they could read, understand, and give a "reasonable interpretation" of any given section of the state's constitution. The government employee giving the test could decide on the section. What's more, this registrar had complete freedom to interpret the test results however he or she wanted. Most black Mississippians received the same result: failed. The state also decided voters should pay a two-dollar **poll tax**, equivalent to about fifteen dollars today. The fees were a real hardship for the state's many poor residents, black and white.

A legal challenge to these requirements eventually reached the Supreme Court, which ruled that the voting tests were fair because they required *all* voters to be able to read, whether black or white. Similarly, the court did not take issue with poll taxes.

After that Supreme Court ruling, other states followed Mississippi's lead. Between 1890 and 1910, every state in the Deep South put in place literacy tests and poll taxes—measures that today are known as "voter suppression." The new rules, as intended, drastically reduced the number of black citizens eligible to vote. For example, in Louisiana in 1896, there were 130,334 registered black voters. Just eight years later, there were only 1,342 African Americans registered to vote in the Pelican State.

A journalist named Jack H. Pollack traveled through the South to investigate the issue, and in 1947, he reported some of his findings:

> “
>
> *A South Carolina Negro decided to memorize the entire Federal and State Constitutions—with all the punctuation. Though he finally came to know both documents far better than his examiners, he was turned down because the registrar was permitted, under his broad powers, to insist that the Constitution be recited in Chinese.*

Pollack pointed out something interesting: the voting test failure rates were high even though the literacy rates for blacks in the South had grown steadily:

> “
>
> *Although ballot-seekers denied registration on "literacy" grounds can usually appeal to the courts, they rarely if ever do. Among other difficulties, the election is generally over before a decision can be rendered. Negro illiteracy in the*

South has been cut from 95 percent in 1865 to 10 percent in 1940, but you'd never know it from the enormous number of Negroes who have never been able to pass "literacy tests."

Martin Luther King and other civil rights leaders thought voting rights were the key to progress for Southern blacks. King believed that putting "proper public officials" in office was foundational to other progress. At a speech in front of the Lincoln Memorial in Washington in 1957, King exhorted listeners with the need for the ballot:

"

All types of conniving methods are still being used to prevent Negroes from becoming registered voters. The denial of this sacred right is a tragic betrayal of the highest mandates of our democratic tradition. And so our most urgent request to the president of the United States and every member of Congress is to give us the right to vote.

Give us the ballot, and we will no longer have to worry the federal government about our basic rights.

Give us the ballot, and we will no longer plead to the federal government for passage of an anti-lynching law; we will by the power of our vote write the law on the statute books of the

South and bring an end to the dastardly acts of the hooded perpetrators of violence.

Winning voting rights and ending segregation would be the two primary goals of peaceful protesters in the civil rights movement.

The Montgomery Bus Boycott

The first successful African American bus boycott occurred in 1953, in Baton Rouge, Louisiana. The eight-day boycott resulted in first-come, first-served seating for all riders, though the two front seats would still be reserved for whites only. Unlike the Montgomery bus boycott, it didn't help bring about a favorable Supreme Court decision. But it was an important example that united action could improve life for blacks in the South.

In 1955, African Americans made up 70 to 75 percent of bus customers on the Montgomery City Lines buses. To ride, they had to (1) pay the driver up front, (2) get off the bus, and (3) re-enter through the rear door. Sometimes bus drivers would simply drive away once the rider got off to re-enter. Black riders had to give up seats whenever white passengers would be otherwise left standing. They often stood huddled in the back while whites comfortably sat. If the back was filled but the front wasn't, black passengers had to stand looking at rows of empty seats.

According to a February 18, 1957, article in *Time*, "At worst, the Negroes were cursed, slapped and kicked by the white drivers." In fact, things could be much worse. In one Montgomery case, a black rider named Hilliard Brooks argued with the bus driver and then the police about getting his ten-cent bus fare back because the back of the bus was filled. During the incident, a policeman shot and killed him.

Civil rights activist Jo Ann Robinson talked about being on a bus in Montgomery. Rushing to the airport with packages in her arms, she had sat in the first rows of a city bus without thinking about what she was doing. The driver walked up to her and raised his arm as if to strike her. "Get up from there!" he shouted, prompting her to run out of the bus. "I felt like a dog," she said in the book *Eyes on the Prize*. "And I got mad, after this was over. I realized that I was a human being and just as intelligent and far more [educationally] trained than that bus driver ... I cried all the way to Cleveland." She would go on to be a critical part of the bus boycott. After Rosa Parks's arrest, Robinson stayed up all night mimeographing thirty-five thousand fliers. The fliers told riders to boycott buses for one day: "We are ... asking every Negro to stay off the buses Monday in protest of the arrest and trial. Don't ride the buses to work, to town, to school or anywhere on Monday."

Martin Luther King Jr. worried over that weekend about whether Montgomery's black citizens would participate in the boycott. But when he and Coretta looked out their kitchen window Monday morning, they saw empty buses passing, and were elated. "Montgomery Negroes," said *Time*, had "walked, rode mules, drove horse-drawn buggies, traveled to work in private cars."

With the boycott, the activists had three demands: (1) courteous treatment by bus drivers, (2) the hiring of more black drivers, and (3) first-come, first-served seating from back to front. They didn't demand access to the front because they were trying to work within the existing law. The place to fight against segregated seating altogether was in the courts, King believed.

More than 150 people volunteered their cars to take boycotters to and from work. The Montgomery Improvement Association (MIA), headed by King, set up nearly 100 stations where people could wait for the cars. Eventually, the MIA received cash donations from all around the world—even as far as Tokyo—and bought station wagons. They painted the names of churches on the car panels, and the vehicles became known as "rolling churches."

As the weeks passed and the boycott continued, city whites grew frustrated. In February—about three months into the boycott—membership in the White Citizens' Council doubled from six thousand to twelve thousand. Martin and Coretta received phone calls from anonymous, irate whites every night. One night, Coretta was home with her baby and heard a thud on the porch. She moved to the back of the house, and a few seconds later an explosion ripped through the living room. Someone had thrown a stick of dynamite onto the Kings' porch.

There would be other bombings, of churches and other activists' homes, including the home of a white Lutheran minister who supported integration. Through it all, King continued to preach nonviolence. "If you truly love and respect an opponent, you respect his fears too," he said.

Eventually, a grand jury indicted King and eighty-nine other boycott participants on charges related to an old law against boycotting. The indictment became national news, and Americans outside Montgomery were introduced more fully to Dr. Martin Luther King Jr. His reputation had already been on the rise. After he was released, King began speaking around the country.

Just as city officials were trying to make it illegal for the people to gather on street corners waiting for rides, word started to spread of something momentous. The Supreme Court, acting on a case filed by the NAACP, had ruled that bus segregation was unconstitutional. The date was November 15, 1956. After 381 days of staying off the city buses, the black citizens of Montgomery had won.

In all, as many as fifty thousand people had participated. The campaign had inspired other boycotts, in Birmingham, Mobile, and Tallahassee. The black churches had become better organized and decided to form the **Southern Christian Leadership Conference (SCLC),** with Dr. King as its head. The SCLC would play a huge role in the civil rights movement. Rosa Parks would emerge as a national icon of peaceful resistance; in 2013, she even had a postage stamp issued in her honor.

After a year of sacrifice and lots of worn-out shoes, black people had not only emerged victorious, they had proved that peaceful protests could help win constitutional rights. Equally important for the movement, Martin Luther King Jr. emerged as a national figure.

Rosa Parks today is a symbol of peaceful and courageous resistance to injustice. Here, she is seated on an integrated bus.

BULL CONNOR

Theophilus Eugene "Bull" Connor rode the tide of Southern white bigotry to a long career in Birmingham politics. Early on, he

was a popular radio sports announcer, and he used his popularity to win a seat in Alabama's legislature. As a state representative, he voted to extend the poll taxes that kept many blacks from voting. Then he became Birmingham's public safety commissioner, in charge of police and fire departments. Throughout his twenty-two years in that office, he enforced segregation with a brutality that was shocking even by the standards of the time. In 1961, he supposedly told members of the KKK that they could have fifteen minutes (uninterrupted by police) to beat up the **Freedom Riders** when their buses pulled into Birmingham. In 1962, he shut down the city's public parks rather than desegregate them. When the Children's Crusade had Birmingham's black children singing and marching in the streets, Connor ordered his men to use high-power fire hoses and police dogs on the young demonstrators–some as young as six.

When the nation saw Connor's tactics, the tide of hatred that had kept Connor in office turned in a direction toward tolerance. His rule as Birmingham's segregation enforcer would end shortly after civil rights activists, led by Martin Luther King Jr., got the city to integrate lunch counters and other spaces. Bull Connor died in 1973 after suffering a stroke.

Dr. King just after a deranged woman stabbed him with a letter opener (protruding from his chest). The woman was institutionalized.

CHAPTER THREE

Nonviolent Resistance

As Dr. King traveled around the country, he talked about Jim Crow realities and civil rights goals and raised funds for civil rights activists. He also wrote a book about the boycott, *Stride Toward Freedom.* In September 1958, he went to a department store in Harlem, a large black neighborhood in New York City, to promote the book and sign autographs. A stylishly dressed black woman in cat eyeglasses approached the table where King sat signing books and asked if he was Martin Luther King. He said he was, and the deranged woman plunged a letter opener into his chest. King was rushed to the hospital, where surgeons performed a risky operation. The knife tip was almost touching his aorta, the body's largest artery, where a puncture would have been fatal. King would later joke that he was happy—and lucky—he hadn't sneezed before the letter opener was removed. The woman who stabbed King, Izola Ware Curry, was found to be insane and later institutionalized. Among other delusions, she thought civil rights leaders were conspiring against her. She died in a nursing home in 2015.

King never expressed any venom toward Curry, only sympathy. He said that he hoped Curry received the help she needed to resume life in society. King's commitments to nonviolence, peace, and love never wavered.

Trip to India

Gandhi was an inspiration to Dr. King.

Shortly after the letter opener attack, King traveled to India with Coretta, to learn more about the nonviolence Gandhi practiced. The trip also gave King a chance to rest after the stabbing and his grueling speaking schedule the year before.

"India's Gandhi was the guiding light of our technique of nonviolent social change," King wrote. He wanted to see for himself how Gandhi's nonviolence had shaped the country. He found the people in India knew about the bus boycott. They showered him with hospitality and, as they loved the old "Negro spirituals" (church songs), often asked Coretta to sing. King spoke at universities and in public meetings, met with leaders including Prime Minister Jawaharlal Nehru, and even found time to take morning walks.

King took home from India a renewed faith that nonviolent revolution yields the greatest results. He said he had seen a spirit of cooperation between Indians and their former British occupiers that was testament to the power of peaceful protest. Of course, passivity doesn't work, he wrote; neither does aggression. "The aftermath of hatred and bitterness that usually follows a violent campaign was found nowhere in India," he wrote. "The way of acquiescence leads to moral and spiritual suicide. The way of violence leads to bitterness in the survivors and brutality in the destroyers. But the way of nonviolence leads to redemption and the creation of the beloved community."

Meeting Hate with Love

Throughout his civil rights career, violence and the threat of violence constantly circled Dr. King. He was tested repeatedly. Just after whites bombed his house during the bus boycott, threatening the lives of his wife and newborn baby, angry men who supported King gathered out in the street. Some had weapons and wanted to retaliate. But King urged the men to stay calm and asked them to remain nonviolent. Even if something were to happen to him, he said, the civil rights movement would go on, and it would succeed.

After the bombing, though, King's father and others in his orbit encouraged him to have armed guards. King did for a time, even applying for a permit to have a gun in the car. Yet ultimately he felt there was a contradiction between being nonviolent and having guns around. He and Coretta talked about it and decided to get rid of the guns. "I was much more afraid in Montgomery when I had a gun in my house," he would write.

> *When I decided that I couldn't keep a gun, I came face-to-face with the question of death and I dealt with it. From that point on, I no longer needed a gun nor have I been afraid. Had we become distracted by the question of my safety we would have lost the moral offensive and sunk to the level of our oppressors.*

King was physically attacked surprisingly often. However, he always chose to "stick with love." An incident during a speech in Birmingham, Alabama, in 1962 is one example of King's true commitment to nonviolence. Authors Mark and Paul Engler describe the scene:

> “
>
> *A 200-pound [90-kilogram] white man, the twenty-four-year-old American Nazi Party member Roy James, jumped onto the stage and struck the clergyman in the face. King responded with a level of courage that made a lifelong impression on many of those in the audience. One of them, storied educator and activist Septima Clark, described how King dropped his hands "like a newborn baby" and spoke calmly to his attacker. King made no effort to protect himself even as he was knocked backwards by further blows.*

King's aides pulled James away from King, who afterward met backstage with the self-described Nazi and said he wouldn't press charges. (James, who was unrepentant, would go to jail, however, after the city pursued charges.) People who witnessed the attack were shocked by the violence, but also by King's response to his assailant and what appeared to be a total lack of fear on King's part.

Sitting In: Youth Step Up

Dr. King was the favored leader and the voice of the civil rights movement, but the movement was diverse and sprawling; it had room for other leaders and for groups besides the SCLC (which King headed). Most important, the civil rights movement included thousands of "regular" people who stood up for change. They made all the difference.

By 1960, the slow pace of change frustrated many young people. *Brown v. Board of Education* had ruled that segregation in schools was unconstitutional and that "separate" was "inherently unequal." But in its effect, the ruling was a bit like a leading domino placed too far from other dominoes to knock any down. The other Jim Crow dominoes—segregation in restaurants, bus terminals, train stations, and other places, and barriers to voting—were still standing. In fact, even school segregation was still a problem. In Greensboro, North Carolina, four freshmen at North Carolina Agricultural and Technical State University stayed up late one night discussing these problems. Ezell Blair Jr., Franklin McCain, Joseph McNeil, and David Richmond, who were later known as the "Greensboro Four," decided to act. On February 1, 1960, they walked into the local Woolworth's department store, purchased sundry items like notebooks and pens, and sat at the whites-only lunch counter. When they asked

The "Greensboro Four" in 1990. This is the same lunch counter at which they were denied service thirty years earlier.

for service, the waitress asked them to leave. The four quietly refused and sat until the store closed. The next day, they returned with more students. The white managers at Woolworth's seemed as if they didn't know what to do. As the sit-in at the Greensboro Woolworth's continued into the days ahead, hundreds of people descended on the store. Some whites came to watch and, in some cases, to harass the young men and women sitting. Others, black and white, came to support the activists.

As the national media picked up the Greensboro story, students in other cities staged lunch counter sit-ins. The best organized of these other groups was in Nashville, Tennessee. These students were from four black colleges in the area and would include future civil rights leaders like the organizer Diane Nash; John Lewis, who would become a US congressman; and Marion Barry, who would become mayor of Washington, DC. On February 13, 1960, the students entered Woolworth's, S. H. Kress, and McClellan stores in Nashville, sat at whites-only counters, and asked for service. The staff in all stores refused. The students would return the next day and in subsequent days. They quickly earned the support of Nashville's African American community, and local clergy called for a boycott of segregated downtown stores.

Sit-in protesters in Nashville and elsewhere practiced how to respond peacefully to harassment. This was important because as the sit-in movement continued, tensions increased. Whites started attacking the students. They poured drinks on the activists, poked them, spit at them, and even put cigarettes out on them. But the activists didn't react. When the police arrested protesters for refusing to leave the whites-only counter, the activists were ready. As soon as a seat at the counter became empty, a new student sat down.

In Nashville, more than eighty students were arrested in one day. A well-known civil rights attorney, Z. Alexander Looby, represented them in court. When Looby made his arguments to the white judge, describing the abuse the students had endured while sitting at the lunch counter, the judge turned his back. Looby gave up, saying "What's the use!" The judge found the students guilty and issued fines.

On April 19, radical whites bombed Looby's house; he and his wife weren't hurt, but the house was destroyed. In response to the bombing, 2,500 Nashville college students and other activists made a silent protest. They marched in organized lines to City Hall. The only noise made was the steady sound of feet hitting pavement. Mayor Ben West met the students outside, and student leader Nash asked West a direct question: Did he think it was wrong to discriminate against someone based on his or her skin color? The mayor said it was wrong.

Segregation in Nashville had taken a fatal blow, and less than one month later, lunch counters in Nashville were integrated. Today, a plaque on the steps of Nashville City Hall quotes a Bible passage: "And the people shouted with a great shout so that the wall fell down."

After a bomb destroyed attorney Z. A. Looby's house, thousands marched, confronting Nashville mayor Ben West.

Back in Greensboro, the Woolworth's would wait until July, summer break, when many students were on vacation, to quietly integrate its lunch counter. A group of female store employees were the first African Americans served.

The sit-in movement brought a new and more confrontational energy into the civil rights movement. In its insistence on "street" action, it was a clear alternative and, perhaps, a challenge to the litigation strategy of the NAACP and older civil rights groups. This previous strategy had relied on cases like *Brown* to bring about change for black citizens. But the students didn't want to wait for the courts to decide segregation was wrong. They had proved they could make change happen without a court ruling.

The next phase of the movement would have students register voters and challenge continued segregation in travel spaces such as train station waiting rooms. With the help of an older NAACP activist named Ella Baker, students organized a new group, the Student Nonviolent Coordinating Committee (SNCC), pronounced "snick."

An Important Phone Call

Not only did the sit-ins help to end segregation in Greensboro, they also influenced the outcome of a presidential election. When Dr. King joined a lunch counter sit-in at a department store in Atlanta, he was arrested, along with 280 students. In the wake of news stories about the jailed protesters, Atlanta's store owners became worried about their image and dropped the charges. The students were released, but King was not, because he was on probation for an earlier traffic violation. The judge sentenced Dr. King to six months' hard labor, with no chance for appeal. Hearing the judge's decision in the courtroom, Coretta broke down in tears. Around 3:00 a.m. that night, jailers took King out of his cell. They chained his arms and tied his legs to the floor in the transport vehicle. King wasn't sure where he was going.

"That kind of mental anguish is worse than dying," he wrote later. "Riding for mile after mile, hungry and thirsty, bound and helpless, waiting and not knowing what you're waiting for. And all over a traffic violation."

When John F. Kennedy, then a candidate for president, heard about Dr. King's predicament, he called Coretta to say he was concerned. Behind the scenes, JFK's brother, Robert Kennedy (who would become the US attorney general after his brother's election) called the judge who had given King such a harsh sentence. He admonished the judge and questioned his judgment. The next day, King was released. King publicly thanked JFK for reaching out to his wife. Many people in the black community took note of the fact that JFK had demonstrated a heart for King, while Richard Nixon, Kennedy's opponent in the presidential campaign, had done nothing. JFK won the

1960 election by a whisper. Many historians believe the black community's vote was critical to JFK's victory; even Nixon said that Kennedy's phone call to Coretta Scott King made the difference.

With influence likes this, Martin Luther King Jr. became even more important on the national scene. "He became the Negro whose name determined a president," said author Taylor Branch in *The King Years.*

Freedom Riders

It now appeared that President Kennedy owed a debt to the black community. Activists were disappointed when he did not immediately send a civil rights bill to Congress. They knew that the Supreme Court had recently ordered bus terminals serving interstate passengers to be integrated. But nothing would change until the ruling body, the Interstate Commerce Commission, ordered bus stations to comply. Thirteen activists working with an organization called the Congress on Racial Equality (CORE) decided to test the waters. Now that Kennedy was president, would he enforce the law? Would he use federal authority and power to force states to protect constitutional rights?

Imagine being on a four-day bus ride and not being able to use a restroom or buy a drink. This was a real possibility facing black passengers in the South. They also had to sit at the back of the bus. The CORE activists planned to ride a bus from Washington, DC, to New Orleans as an interracial group. Whites would sit in the back and blacks in the front. At stations, black activists would order service from whites-only counters and use whites-only facilities. "You will never make it through Alabama," Dr. King warned them.

They called themselves the Freedom Riders. When the first Freedom Rider bus pulled into the Alabama town of Anniston, waiting there was a mob of perhaps two hundred angry white people. The mob threw stones at the bus and slashed the tires. The driver careened away, but whites caught up and firebombed it. Thankfully, all the activists escaped through the emergency exit. The next morning, images of the blazing bus would be on the front pages of newspapers around the country. Meanwhile, the second bus arrived in Birmingham. Commissioner Bull Connor had posted no police protection for the riders, while knowing

The Freedom Riders, here showing fatigue, traveled through the South knowing they would likely be beaten or even killed.

Freedom Riders managed to escape a bus that angry segregationists firebombed in Anniston, Alabama.

there would be trouble. The rumor was that Connor told men in the Klan they would have fifteen minutes "to burn, bomb, kill, maim, I don't give a goddamn." Klansmen boarded the bus and beat up rider Jim Peck as well as Walter Bergman, who would have a stroke less than two weeks later and be in a wheelchair for the rest of his life.

As the students recovered in the hospital, JFK and Robert Kennedy sent their assistant, John Seigenthaler, to intervene in Alabama and calm down tensions if he could. Meanwhile, the bus company did not want to move forward after the attack and firebombing, and James Farmer, the head of CORE, believed continuing was too dangerous, so he ended the campaign.

Phase II

When students in Nashville heard about this, they decided to step in. Seigenthaler learned of the Nashville students' plans to travel to Alabama, and he called Diane Nash. He recalled for a PBS documentary on the Freedom Riders that he loudly exclaimed to her that "people are going to die!"

> "
>
> *And there's a pause, and she said, "Sir, you should know, we all signed our last wills and testaments last night before they left. We know someone will be killed. But we cannot let violence overcome nonviolence."*
>
> *That's virtually a direct quote of the words that came out of that child's mouth.*
>
> *Here I am, an official of the United States government, representing the president and the attorney general, talking to a student at Fisk University. And she, in a very quiet but strong way, gave me a lecture.*

Bull Connor arrested the Nashville students when they arrived in Birmingham, claiming he was putting them in protective custody. While the students were in jail, the White House negotiated with John Patterson, the governor of Alabama, who finally agreed to protect the riders. The Freedom Riders were rushed onto a waiting bus, which hurtled toward Montgomery at high speed. Reporters followed, as did police car escorts and, overhead, a plane from the highway patrol. When the bus got to the

Montgomery line, the police cars fell back and the plane overhead veered off. The bus pulled into an eerily quiet bus terminal. Getting off the bus and starting to speak to reporters, with other Freedom Riders circled behind him, John Lewis said, quietly, "It doesn't look right." Recalling what happened next, another rider, Frederick Leonard, later said, "And then, all of a sudden, just like magic: white people, sticks, and bricks."

The mob didn't seem interested in taking prisoners. They had pipes and chains. One woman hit a female Freedom Rider repeatedly with her handbag. The riders were nonviolent, so they wouldn't fight back, but that didn't stop the attackers. Seigenthaler had stopped nearby

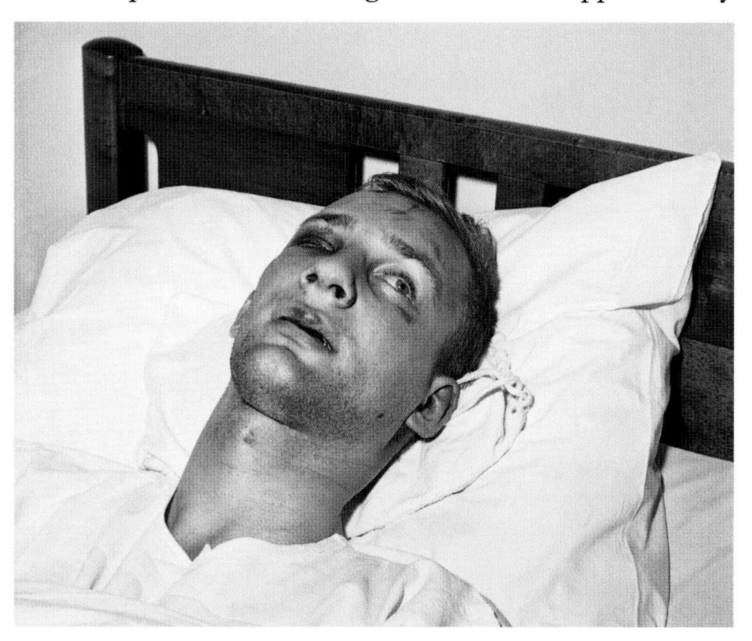

Freedom Rider Jim Zwerg recovers in a hospital after being beaten by a white mob in Montgomery, Alabama.

to get a coffee and heard screams. From the direction of the terminal, he saw luggage flying. He rushed to the scene, pulling up in his car right into the middle of the fracas to break it up. As he tried to help a girl being beaten, someone hit him in the head with a pipe, knocking him unconscious. The mob stopped only when the Alabama state police chief put a gun to the head of a white man, ordering everyone to stop.

That day, JFK sent hundreds of federal marshals to Alabama. If he and his brother had been reluctant to use force against a state, they overcame those hesitations. Perhaps hearing of unchecked violence against peaceful students and seeing their own man lying in the street did away with any doubts they had. (Seigenthaler did recover.)

Outside the Church

King flew to Montgomery to lend his support to the Freedom Riders. "The federal government must not stand idly by while bloodthirsty mobs beat nonviolent students with impunity," he said. While he was speaking to more than one thousand people at his friend and fellow activist Ralph Abernathy's church, a mob of three thousand white people surrounded the church. Even though US marshals guarded the church, the mob was threatening. Eventually, RFK told Governor Patterson he would send in federal troops if the situation continued. Patterson sent in the National Guard, which used tear gas to disperse the people. As the gas seeped into the church, making eyes tear and throats burn, King encouraged the crowd to remain calm. "We are not afraid, and we shall overcome," he said. Later that night, officers escorted King and the others out of the church to safety.

Two days later, twenty-seven riders left Montgomery for Mississippi. This time, when they got to Jackson, there were no mobs. Instead, they were ushered through the whites-only area, out the door, and into a paddy wagon. When the arrested students were tried, this judge, too, turned his back on the defending attorney. He sentenced the activists to sixty days in the state penitentiary. More riders arrived in Jackson. They were arrested, too, yet other riders followed. By the time they were done, three hundred Freedom Riders were arrested and jailed.

On May 29, 1961, RFK directed the Interstate Commerce Commission to ban segregation in all terminals it oversaw; on November 1, the ICC ruled that segregation on buses and in terminals and facilities was illegal. The Freedom Riders had won, although it had been more than tough.

The Freedom Riders would not soon be forgotten in America. And in the South, "Freedom Rider" became a catch-all term for anyone working on civil rights, said Juan Williams in *Eyes on the Prize*. "The courage and tenacity of those pioneers had captured the imagination and awe of blacks throughout the Southland," he wrote.

The Albany Campaign

Toward the end of 1961, Dr. King traveled to southwestern Georgia, where young activists were waging an ambitious, broad effort to challenge Jim Crow in the city of Albany. The organizations involved included SNCC, the NAACP, and, for a time, the SCLC. The Albany Campaign used a variety of nonviolent tactics to achieve its goals. These tactics included sit-ins at the bus station and other places, marches, mass demonstrations, and boycotts.

The Albany sheriff, Laurie Pritchett, did not use public brutality, but he did make arrests. By the time Dr. King arrived, hundreds of activists were in jail. Soon, Dr. King and Ralph Abernathy were in jail, too. They hoped publicity about their imprisonment would help bring about change in Albany, and indeed, the city started negotiating with the activists. Their final agreement stated that if King left Albany, the city would desegregate its bus terminal and release the protesters from jail. However, it turned out the city was not negotiating in good faith. Terminals remained segregated. Arrests and imprisonments continued. Sadly for Dr. King, the media reported the Albany movement as a stunning defeat for him.

Six months later, King and Abernathy, back in Albany for a trial related to their earlier arrest, were convicted of parading without a permit. They refused the option to pay bail, in sympathy for the seven hundred protesters in

Albany who were in jail. An anonymous person, possibly Pritchett himself, bailed them out overnight. Abernathy would quip that it was the first time he had ever been thrown out of jail.

Eventually, Dr. King abandoned the campaign in Albany. "The mistake I made there," he would say, "was to protest against segregation generally rather than against a single and distinct facet of it." In addition, Pritchett had been smart. He refused to be seen using violence (although one activist did get beaten by guards and miscarried her baby), and as a result, the campaign did not have the kinds of dramatic press photos or media attention that often pushed city and state authorities to take positive action. And Pritchett resisted the campaign's plans to "fill up the jails," by spreading prisoners out in jails distributed around Albany. However, the lessons King learned in Albany would teach him better strategies for a new campaign, in Birmingham.

The Birmingham Campaign

In 1963, Birmingham was among the most segregated cities in the South. The city went to great lengths to ensure separation of black and white. Birmingham was also notorious for bombings against African Americans. In fact, the city had a nickname: "Bombingham." The city's record of police brutality, said Dr. King, "is known in every section of this country ... Its unjust treatment of Negroes in the courts is a notorious reality."

After the disappointing results in Albany, King wanted a local civil rights campaign that would advance the fight for equality. He wanted a success. "We believed that while a campaign in Birmingham would surely be the toughest fight of our civil rights careers, it could, if successful, break the back of segregation all over the nation," King wrote. In Albany, the activists had mobilized an effort that was perhaps too broad. Now, the campaign decided to focus on a slice of Birmingham society: the businesses. They would demonstrate in the city during the second-biggest shopping season of the year, Easter. King and his team decided to refer to the campaign as Project C, with the "C" standing for "confrontation."

The campaign used a boycott of downtown merchants, as well as mass demonstrations, marches, and lunch counter sit-ins. Hundreds of activists were arrested. Bull Connor, the city's head of public safety—a position above the sheriff—was notoriously brutish. But now, Connor and the Birmingham law were using surprisingly little violence to manage the protests. King wondered what was going on.

In fact, the city had asked a state circuit court to stop all protests; eventually it won this injunction. The city's officials were trying to simply shut the movement down. King had never disobeyed a court order. But this time,

Dr. King was arrested many times because of his civil disobedience. Here he is pictured in the Jefferson County Jail in Alabama.

he and Abernathy stepped out. On Good Friday, the two men joined fifty other people in a march in Birmingham, and they were arrested. In solitary confinement for part of his imprisonment, King wrote a letter that would become one of his most famous writings.

Letter from Birmingham Jail

King's letter responded to criticism about the Birmingham Campaign from local clergy. These clergymen wrote an open letter urging African Americans of Birmingham not to participate in demonstrations but instead to work "peacefully for a better Birmingham." They argued that the Birmingham Campaign was poorly timed because the city had just elected a new mayor committed to improving life for blacks, and they suggested Dr. King was an outsider interfering in Birmingham's civil rights progress.

King's response was very long, in part because he was in jail for eight days and had a lot of time to work on it. Yet he probably also knew he was writing a letter in the tradition of Thoreau's essay on civil disobedience, a letter that would be remembered. At first, King had to write the letter in the margins of newspapers because he didn't have paper. Eventually, a jailer gave him a pad. In his letter, King pointed out that he was not an interloper because the SCLC had member churches in Birmingham; in addition, he wrote, area civil rights leaders had asked him to come. In response to the charge that he should give the new mayor time to make changes, King pointed out that the new mayor was a segregationist. "We have not made a single gain in civil rights without determined legal and nonviolent pressure," he wrote. As for the plea to wait until the time was "right," King said:

"

We know through painful experience that freedom is never voluntarily given by the oppressor; it must be demanded by the oppressed. Frankly, I have yet to engage in a direct action campaign that was "well timed" in the view of those who have not suffered unduly from the disease of segregation. For years now I have heard the word "Wait!" It rings in the ear of every Negro with piercing familiarity. This "Wait" has almost always meant "Never."

Referring to efforts in other countries to overthrow colonial rulers, he said: "The nations of Asia and Africa are moving with jetlike speed toward gaining political independence, but we still creep at horse and buggy pace toward gaining a cup of coffee at a lunch counter."

King continued the letter by talking about all the reasons for civil rights nonviolent direct action. He also mentioned that he was increasingly disappointed in the response—or lack of response—from white moderate people. Moderates claimed to be sympathetic to the plight of blacks under Jim Crow, but King believed they did not back up their words with action. "I have almost reached the regrettable conclusion that the Negro's great stumbling block in his stride toward freedom is not the White Citizen's Councillor or the Ku Klux Klanner, but the white moderate," he wrote, "who is more devoted to 'order' than to justice."

The letter is also a hopeful one. "Oppressed people cannot remain oppressed forever," King wrote. "The yearning for freedom eventually manifests itself, and that is what has happened to the American Negro. Something within has reminded him of his birthright of freedom, and something without has reminded him that it can be gained."

"Letter from Birmingham Jail" was initially distributed as a mimeographed copy, then published over the succeeding months and years in several magazines, and finally submitted into the Congressional Record. It is today taught widely in schools and regarded as an example of fine rhetorical writing and a significant piece of civil rights argument and history.

Children's Crusade

When King got out of jail, he and the other campaign leaders felt they needed to intensify the campaign. Activist James Bevel had an idea: What if they had the children of Birmingham march? The children would not only bring a "dramatic new dimension" to the story unfolding in Birmingham, they would benefit from claiming a stake in the fight for freedom, he argued. King supported this idea. "We found [the children] eager to belong, hungry for participation in a significant social effort," King said.

The world was shocked to see images like this one come out of Birmingham during the Children's Crusade to end segregation.

FREEDOM SUMMER

In spring 1964, Congress was about to pass a civil rights bill, and the nation was reeling from the assassination of President Kennedy. But the black community didn't lose focus on the goal of securing voting rights. Young activists in Mississippi were especially eager to make headway. Although the state was about 45 percent African American, Mississippi had the lowest percentage of registered black voters. Some counties did not have a single black voter on the rolls.

That summer, more than one thousand young people, mostly white and from the North, took part in the Mississippi Summer Project, later known as Freedom Summer. They worked with black Mississippi volunteers toward several goals:

1. Register black voters.
2. Help create a "Mississippi Freedom Democratic Party" as an alternative to the Democratic Party in Mississippi, which was all white and favored segregation.
3. Establish Freedom Schools to teach basic skills, black history, and civil rights.
4. Establish health clinics and legal clinics.

Most of the students participating were from comparatively wealthy families. To participate, they had to bring $500 in bail-out cash, for they were likely to be arrested. They also had to pay for living expenses. Many Mississippi whites resented the sudden presence of one thousand rich, Northern young people. Before the summer was over, activists would be beaten (eighty of them) and arrested (one thousand), and scores of black churches would be burned.

But the most tragic retaliation was murder. James Chaney, a local volunteer, and two activists, Andrew Goodman, and Michael Schwerner, disappeared on the second day. It would be weeks before authorities would find their bodies in a shallow grave. The FBI later figured out the three had been arrested, briefly jailed, and then forced over on the road after being released. All three had been shot by Klansmen. During the search, authorities also found the bodies of other black men and boys who had gone missing. Herbert Oarsby was fourteen and was reportedly wearing a CORE T-shirt. Charles Eddie Moore had participated in civil rights protests and was killed with his friend Henry Hezekiah Dee. Five other bodies were never identified.

Despite this tragedy, the Freedom Summer volunteers soldiered on. By the time they were done, they had set up fifty Freedom Schools that taught more than 3,500 students of all ages, even the elderly. These schools would be a model for future programs like the very successful Head Start Program. They had also registered between 1,200 and 1,600 new black voters.

On May 2, more than a thousand students converged on the streets of downtown Birmingham. Hundreds were arrested, which shocked people around the world. The next day, hundreds more students gathered. This time, Bull Connor ordered his officers to get tough. The police let their German shepherd dogs loose on the children, who were mostly high schoolers but also included children as young as six. The officers sprayed the children with high-pressure fire hoses, sending some of them tumbling down the street in the projectiles of water. With some students, police even used their billy clubs.

Appallingly, the city put up to seventy-five students in jail cells meant for far fewer. For the first time, King said while speaking to the press, they had been able to fulfill the Gandhian principle of effective nonviolent action: "filling up the jails."

The horrifying scenes coming out of Birmingham—children getting jailed, assaulted with fire hoses, and bitten by dogs—were too much for the world. It seemed as if the civil rights struggle hit a tipping point; people all over had enough and started to act on their own. The media reacted as well. Historian Taylor Branch would point out that the *New York Times* published more stories about race in the two weeks after the start of the Children's Crusade than it did the entire previous year. King left Birmingham with the campaign still going to raise publicity and funds, and he began a whirlwind tour of speaking stops. These included the first white mass meeting related to civil rights, in Cleveland. In Chicago, there was a concert and rally featuring the likes of Mahalia Jackson, Diana Ross, and the up-and-coming Aretha Franklin. Around the country, people started marching and demonstrating spontaneously for civil rights.

Even Bull Connor's men appeared to be changing. According to King, on one Saturday afternoon, when several hundred protesters marched, Bull Connor ordered his men to "turn on the hoses." The marchers had been heading to a prayer meeting. "What happened in the next thirty seconds was one of the most fantastic events of the Birmingham story," King wrote.

"

Bull Connor's men stood facing the marchers. The marchers, many of them on their knees … stared back, unafraid and unmoving. Slowly the Negroes stood up and began to advance. Connor's men, as though hypnotized, fell back, their hoses sagging uselessly in their hands while several hundred Negroes marched past them.

Meanwhile, in Washington, JFK was paying attention to civil rights battles around the country. He heard Governor George Wallace of Alabama declare, "Segregation now, segregation tomorrow, segregation forever!" He read King's "Letter from Birmingham Jail." He eventually sent a man to Birmingham to help negotiate a deal between the campaign and the city political and business leaders; the deal they reached called for the city to integrate lunch counters and other facilities, to provide more jobs for African Americans, and to set up a committee that would investigate any complaints of injustice brought by black people. Most important, he made a televised speech calling for new civil rights legislation.

A new day was dawning in Birmingham, but segregationists were enraged. The night the agreement was announced, a bomb went off in the motel where King and SCLC leaders had been staying. Fortunately, they were not at the hotel that night. Another bomb went off at the Birmingham home of Dr. King's brother, A. D. In response to the unrest, JFK ordered three thousand federal troops into Birmingham to restore and keep order.

Four Little Girls

Four months after the Birmingham deal was announced, the city was still struggling to come to terms with desegregation. Violence was not over. The worst of it came on September 15, when KKK members planted a bomb under a stairwell at the Sixteenth Street Baptist Church. This historic church was a symbol of the civil rights movement in Birmingham and had been a launching

The pastor of Birmingham's Sixteenth Street Baptist Church, Rev. John Cross, after the infamous bombing that killed four girls there

point for many of the summer protests. The bomb went off just as four girls, three of them fourteen years old and one of them eleven years old, were walking down the stairwell over the explosive. They were all killed. These girls, Addie Mae Collins, Denise McNair, Carole Robertson, and Cynthia Wesley, "unoffending, innocent and beautiful, were the victims of one of the most vicious, heinous crimes every perpetrated against humanity," Dr. King said at their joint funeral. Their murders helped lead to the passage of the **Civil Rights Act of 1964**, which would outlaw segregation once and for all.

After his "I Have a Dream" speech to the crowd seen here in Washington, DC, Dr. King "stepped down on the other side of history," said Clarence Jones.

CHAPTER FOUR

The Effects of the Civil Rights Movement

The March on Washington for Jobs and Freedom took place shortly before the Sixteenth Street Baptist Church bombing, on August 28, 1963, a hot but not terribly humid summer day in Washington, DC. The march organizers hoped as many as 100,000 people would show, but before the day was over, 250,000 people would be in attendance.

Performers included singers Mahalia Jackson and Marian Anderson, as well as folk singers Joan Baez and Bob Dylan. Speakers included march organizers A. Philip Randolph and Bayard Rustin, NAACP president Roy Wilkins, and SNCC leader John Lewis. Milling about in the crowd were stars such as Sidney Poitier, Sammy Davis Jr., and Harry Belafonte, a frequent supporter of the civil rights movement. Even singer Josephine Baker attended, having traveled from France. Also present was an American hero of a different kind: Jackie Robinson, the man who broke the color barrier in Major League Baseball.

Reports of the day say that the crowd's enthusiasm was waning after several long, hot, crowded hours on the Mall (the stretch of grass, pavement, and a reflecting pool between the US Capitol and the Lincoln Memorial). King was the last speaker on the program.

He had a prepared speech that was perfectly fine, but this was his moment. America was watching, and Dr. King had the opportunity to give a speech would help catapult him to a new position from which to fight for rights for his people.

Mahalia Jackson was seated behind King on the stage. As he spoke, she said, "Tell them about the dream, Martin!" King put aside his written speech. His stance changed. He was moving into preacher mode. He spoke of a dream "deeply rooted in the American dream," and said he hoped that one day "this nation will rise up and live out the true meaning of its creed: 'We hold these truths to be self-evident, that all men are created equal.'" The crowd was with him, answering and applauding.

With a preacher's cadence, he said he wanted freedom to ring from "every hill and molehill of Mississippi." He

Dr. King delivering his "I Have a Dream" speech in 1963

dreamed of the day when "little black boys and black girls will be able to join hands with little white boys and white girls as sisters and brothers."

The audience was his now. He ended by hoping for the day when all people could "join hands and sing in the words of the old Negro spiritual: 'Free at last! Free at last! Thank God Almighty, we are free at last!'" The audience roared with approval, and the men and women behind King on the platform crowded around, slapping him on the back to congratulate him.

Dr. King was a prominent figure before the speech, King's adviser Clarence Jones would say later, but after the "I Have a Dream" speech, King had "stepped down on the other side of history." King himself would say of the March on Washington:

> "
>
> *Millions of white Americans, for the first time, had a clear, long look at Negroes engaged in a serious occupation. For the first time millions listened to the informed and thoughtful words of Negro spokesmen, from all walks of life. The stereotype of the Negro suffered a heavy blow … As television beamed the image of this extraordinary gathering across the border oceans, everyone who believed in man's capacity to better himself had a moment of inspiration and confidence in the future of the human race. And every dedicated American could be proud that a dynamic experience of democracy in the nation's capital had been made visible to the world."*

President Lyndon Johnson would sign the Civil Rights Act of 1964 on July 2. It prohibited discrimination based on race, color, religion, sex, or national origin, and strengthened prohibitions on segregation in schools and discrimination in voting registration.

Martin Luther King Jr. was there when President Johnson signed the Civil Rights Act of 1964.

Dr. King was at Johnson's side as he signed the act into law. In terms of time passed, it was eight months after the assassination of JFK, who had introduced the bill; ten months after the bombing at the Sixteenth Street Baptist Church; eleven months after the March on Washington; more than a year after the Birmingham Campaign; more than two years since the Albany Campaign; more than three years since the Freedom Riders first traveled South; more than four years since the first lunch counter sit-ins; and almost ten years since the Montgomery bus boycott.

Fighting On

The Civil Rights Act of 1964 was a credit to the determination, fortitude, and grit of people seeking only their basic rights. Although there was tremendous pressure on JFK and then President Johnson to make the Civil Rights Act a reality, historians give them credit, too, because they responded to the call for justice. (JFK was assassinated before Congress passed his bill. Johnson took it up once he became president.) But many people, including Dr. King, thought the Civil Rights Act didn't go far enough. They wanted a law that specifically prohibited the tactics used in the South to keep blacks from voting. Without free access to the voting booth, argued King, the black community would forever have second-class status.

Dr. King and the civil rights community were determined to see the job done. The fight for rights would continue. King and others in the movement were about to make the name Selma a shorthand for the courageous civil rights struggle and the Southern states' use of brute force to resist.

Selma

As we've seen, the Fifteenth Amendment, which granted African American men the legal right to vote, didn't seem to matter in the South. Nearly one hundred years after states had ratified that amendment, few blacks in the South had been given the franchise. In 1963 in Selma, Alabama, 156 of 15,000 black people were registered to vote. The registrar's office was open only a couple of days out of every month. Often people would have to take off work to try to register, meaning their employers might find out and retaliate. Bruce Hartford, an Alabama civil rights worker, says on his website:

> *On the occasional registration day, the county sheriff and his deputies made it their business to hang around the courthouse to discourage "undesirables" from trying to register. This meant that black women and men had to run a gauntlet of intimidation, insults, threats, and sometimes arrest on phony charges, just to get to the registration office. Once in the registrar's office they faced hatred, harassment, and humiliation from clerks and officials.*

The student organization SNCC was active in Selma, trying to integrate theaters and lunch counters, and promoting voter registration through voter registration days. King and his team were looking for a place to work that would provide the headlines they needed. They knew the Selma sheriff, Jim Clark, was a violent man who wouldn't react well to civil disobedience such as mass demonstrations and protest marches. They felt certain that Clark's response to nonviolent protest would attract media attention and reveal the violent side of voter suppression. Clark was known to blacks as a notorious racist, and King hoped publicity would pressure Lyndon Johnson to put forth voting rights legislation. The president didn't want to do so in part because he had just helped bring about the Civil Rights Act. He worried about negative reaction, especially in the South, hurting his other programs. But black people didn't want to wait. King felt the time to act was "now." In January 1965, King and the SCLC joined SNCC in conducting civil rights work in Selma.

When King led people to the Selma courthouse to demand access to register to vote, Sheriff Clark told the demonstrators to wait in an alley. They waited all day, but no one was brought in to register. The next day, King led more marchers to the courthouse. This time, they refused to wait in the alley. When one woman, Amelia Boynton, "stepped out of line," Clark grabbed her and shoved her down the street. Cameras clicked, and photos of Clark arresting Boynton made the news pages the next day. When people surged into the courthouse, Clark arrested them.

One day, the Selma teachers marched, and the rest of the city knew the African Americans of Selma were serious. The teachers were usually conservative in activism

Activists help a woman beaten during the Bloody Sunday protest in Selma, Alabama, while an officer looks on.

because they could lose their jobs—and then who would teach the children? But now, there were the teachers, marching and waving toothbrushes in the air to show they were willing to be arrested.

When police came to break up a line of demonstrators one day, Clark pushed a billy club into a fifty-six-year-old demonstrator's neck. Annie Lee Cooper turned around and slugged him; some reports say she managed to hit him in the face three times, and with strong punches, too. She was arrested and released, but photos in the newspapers the next day made Clark look bad.

As the days passed, King decided to up the ante. He led a march of hundreds through Selma that was in violation of anti-parade laws; additional marches, including one by three hundred children, started to fill up Selma's jails. The nation was watching, and eventually the situation in Selma prompted a delegation of congressmen to travel there to investigate.

Bloody Sunday

At a nighttime march in nearby Marion, Alabama, on February 18, tragedy struck. The streetlights went out, and suddenly the marchers were running to escape the batons of state troopers and local police. One twenty-six-year-old man, Jimmie Lee Jackson, a church deacon and former soldier, tried to protect his mother from a policeman's blows and was fatally shot.

Responding to Jimmie Lee Jackson's death, activists set out on March 7 to march from Selma to the state capitol in Montgomery, about 50 miles (80 km) away. Carrying bedrolls and other belongings, the marchers met a phalanx of troopers and police just over the rise on the Edmund Pettus Bridge. The troopers had gas masks hanging from their belts. The crowd didn't disperse when ordered, and the officers, including some on horseback, flew into the crowd, swinging clubs and throwing tear gas canisters. TV crews were there, meaning Bloody Sunday, as it came to be known, was televised for all to see. Much of the nation was horrified.

After people were tended to and wounds bandaged, King sent a telegram to clergy around the country asking them to travel to Selma and join the fight. That Tuesday, 1,500 people, led by King, marched again across the Edmund Pettus Bridge. Again, they met a phalanx of troopers and police. The marchers stopped, started singing "We Shall Overcome," and knelt to pray. Then, to everyone's surprise, King turned around and led everyone back whence they came. King would later say he didn't want more casualties. He felt he had made the necessary point about the dangers facing people who were only trying to exercise their rights.

Later that night in Selma, two white ministers were attacked as they left an integrated restaurant. James Reeb, a Unitarian Universalist minister from Boston, was badly beaten and two days later died of head injuries. President Johnson called Reeb's death a national tragedy. Many people now felt the injustice in the South was a nightmare and wanted it to end.

That Monday night, President Johnson went to Congress and on live television announced new voting rights legislation. He asked Americans to engage in the fight. "Their cause must be our cause too. Because it is not just Negroes, but really it is all of us who must overcome the crippling legacy of bigotry and injustice. And we *shall* overcome," he said.

The next day, a judge ruled that the demonstrators had a right to march from Selma to Montgomery without interference. About four thousand people gathered for the trek, but by the time the marched neared Montgomery, there would be twenty-five thousand. When they reached the capitol building in Montgomery, Martin Luther King spoke to the crowd. "The end we seek is a society at peace with itself, a society that can live with its conscience," he said. "And that will be a day not of the white man, not of the black man. That will be the day of man as man."

On August 6 at the White House, Johnson signed the **Voting Rights Act of 1965**, which prohibited state and local voting laws resulting in discrimination against racial or other minorities. It specifically outlawed literacy tests.

Black voter turnout in the South would grow steadily after 1965. More than forty years later, Barack Obama

The march from Selma to Montgomery included twenty-five thousand participants, among them Dr. King.

ran for president in 2008 and again in 2012, and the rate of black voting in the South was greater than the rate anywhere else in the country.

Poor People's Campaign

In August 1965, a six-day riot in the poor Los Angeles neighborhood of Watts ended in thirty-four dead, as many as one thousand people injured, and millions of dollars' worth of damage. The Watts riot—sometimes called the Watts Rebellion—and riots in other cities were an outgrowth of the country's failure to address poverty, King believed. An official inquiry into the Watts riot seemed to reach the same conclusion: Watts residents were tired of being jobless, living in substandard housing, and going to underfunded schools.

When King toured the Watts neighborhood, the anger people felt at the inequality around them was apparent. There were many who loved and revered Dr. King, but there were others who thought violence, rather than nonviolence, was the best response. This debate had intensified in the black community in recent years. Calls for "Black Power" and a more militant approach were on the rise.

The new social justice battleground would have to be in the realm of "dignity and work," King said, as opposed to fighting for basic rights as the SCLC had done in the

South. According to biographer David J. Garrow, King told Bayard Rustin, "I worked to get these people the right to eat hamburgers, and now I've got to do something … to help them get the money to buy it."

King moved his family to Chicago so he could be immersed in the lives of the people he wanted to serve. He would be tackling the problems of "de facto" segregation: segregation that was not codified into laws but nevertheless existed. Chicago didn't have Jim Crow laws, but just like in Los Angeles, it had black ghettos and high unemployment for blacks, who faced discrimination when they looked for housing and work. In many ways, these problems were less easily solved.

King worked with SCLC workers already active in Chicago, including a young Jesse Jackson, to fight against

Dr. King's friend and fellow activist Ralph Abernathy (*right of center*) leads a Poor People's Campaign march in the summer of 1968.

discrimination and poverty. Eventually he announced a new campaign—the **Poor People's Campaign**—a name that reminds us of the concern he felt about poverty and inequity when he was only five years old and saw people in a breadline. The campaign was also the brainchild of Marian Wright, then director of the NAACP Legal Defense and Education Fund in Jackson, Mississippi. (Today she is a leading advocate for children and heads the Children's Defense Fund, which she founded.) The campaign used nonviolence and direct actions such as marches and protests to draw attention to poverty and economic injustice. It reached beyond the black community, as leaders from the American Indian, Mexican American, white, and other communities pledged their support.

The launch of the Poor People's Campaign, King said, "is the beginning of a new co-operation, understanding, and a determination by poor people of all colors and backgrounds to assert and win their right to a decent life and respect for their culture and dignity."

In this later period of his life, King also spoke out strongly against the Vietnam War. Of course, this was a consistent position for anyone who practiced nonviolence, but it earned Dr. King criticism and the enmity of President Johnson. There were even some civil rights leaders who disavowed King's stance on the war.

In a now famous speech at Riverside Church in New York City—a year to the day before his assassination—

King spoke strongly about the injustice of the war, and the opportunity to turn the tide of history toward peace and justice.

"

> *Somehow this madness must cease. We must stop now. I speak as a child of God and brother to the suffering poor of Vietnam. I speak for those whose land is being laid waste, whose homes are being destroyed, whose culture is being subverted. I speak for the poor of America who are paying the double price of smashed hopes at home and death and corruption in Vietnam. I speak as a citizen of the world, for the world as it stands aghast at the path we have taken. I speak as an American to the leaders of my own nation. The great initiative in this war is ours. The initiative to stop it must be ours.*

What Would Dr. King Say?

With the Poor People's Campaign, Martin Luther King not only moved his center of activity out of the rural South, he was now asking America to confront thorny problems whose roots were economic and whose solutions were less immediately apparent. Fighting for income equality can make a person unpopular, even someone beloved like

King, because it involves how people's money gets spent as taxes, how much people should be taxed, and whether some people have too much money or aren't paying their fair share of taxes.

Some people argue that as Dr. King has become glorified, his more challenging, less popular message has been smoothed out. They say people remember his work against flagrant racial injustices but forget his consistent positions against economic injustice. These people work to remind us of Dr. King's later activism through the Poor People's Campaign.

Dr. King's words about economic justice are echoed today by politicians, opinion makers, and community groups that seek to end poverty, child hunger, and homelessness. In fact, his words are a close match to some of the arguments we hear today. In a speech called "The Other America," King said:

"

One America is flowing with the milk of prosperity and the honey of equality. That America is the habitat of millions of people who have food and material necessities for their bodies, culture and education for their minds, freedom and human dignity for their spirits ... But as we assemble here tonight, I'm sure that each of us is painfully aware of the fact that there is another

America, and that other America has a daily ugliness about it that transforms the buoyancy of hope into the fatigue of despair.

King's Death

Dr. King traveled to Memphis, Tennessee, in April 1968 to participate in a march in support of striking sanitation workers. He stayed at the Lorraine Motel, where he was a frequent guest. On April 4, at about 6:00 p.m., he stepped out onto the balcony of his second-story room to speak to his friends in the parking lot below. Suddenly there was a shot, and King was thrown back. The bullet had struck Dr. King in his chin and neck. As King lay wounded on the balcony floor, Ralph Abernathy cradled King's head. King was rushed to the hospital by ambulance, but he was pronounced dead at 7:05 p.m.

The sad scene at the Lorraine Motel, as Dr. King's body was taken from the balcony to the hospital

King's last words, according to writer and historian Taylor Branch, had been about his favorite gospel song. Ben Branch, a saxophonist who was set to perform at an event featuring King later that night, was outside in the parking lot when King stepped out on the balcony. King supposedly said, "Ben, make sure you play 'Take My Hand, Precious Lord' in the meeting tonight. Play it real pretty."

President Johnson declared April 7, 1968, a day of national mourning. People around the world watched King's televised funeral procession through the streets of Atlanta. Two mules pulled his coffin, which was followed by tens of thousands of mourners.

A Haunting Photo

When Coretta learned that there were no black photographers set to take photos at her husband's funeral, she insisted on including a photographer who had often taken photos of Dr. King. Not only would Moneta Sleet take poignant photos of Coretta and her children during the service, but one of his images would go on to make him the first black man to win a Pulitzer Prize. The award-winning image shows a veiled, grief-stricken Coretta holding in her lap daughter Bernice, staring into the distance with a haunting look of having been forsaken.

The man arrested and convicted for the killing, James Earl Ray, plead guilty but later reversed his guilty

MARTIN LUTHER KING JR. AND CIVIL RIGHTS COMMEMORATED

Martin Luther King Jr.'s impact on the world is hard to overstate. In addition to leading a movement that brought about an end to segregation and Jim Crow–era voter suppression, he popularized nonviolence as an approach to seeking political change. He provided a model for protest that thrives today in continued efforts for civil rights, movements for gay and transgender rights, and protests on issues including the environment and police brutality.

Americans take a holiday in honor of Dr. King every year, and it's one of the few holidays in the nation that commemorates a single

This 30-foot (9.1-meter) granite statue of Dr. King is the centerpiece of the Martin Luther King Jr. Memorial in Washington, DC.

individual. Dr. King's birthday is, in fact, celebrated worldwide, and there are streets, monuments, and parks all over the globe named after Martin Luther King Jr.

He has become an icon for the United States civil rights movement and for freedom struggles everywhere. During the Arab Spring of 2011, young people filled Tahrir Square in Cairo, Egypt, as part of that country's democratic uprising. They had learned how to conduct peaceful protests from reprints of *Montgomery Story* comic books, which a nonprofit group had translated into Arabic and Farsi. Decades earlier, in pro-democracy protests by young people in China's Tiananmen Square, protesters held signs that read "We Shall Overcome," a promise used repeatedly during the civil rights movement. When Nelson Mandela won South Africa's first free election, he cited Dr. King and used his words: "Free at Last."

Today's leaders, including Barack Obama and Hillary Clinton, were all influenced by Martin Luther King—as have been countless others. "Growing up," said actor Forest Whitaker, "Dr. Martin Luther King Jr. was the one photograph that every black household had. There were little placards made out of metal stuck against the wall. You followed him because he was holding your hope. The hope that you were going to be able to live your life full with equality."

admission. King's own family came to believe Ray was innocent and asked for further investigation. Eventually, the government said there may have been coconspirators, but there was no evidence of government involvement in King's death.

King's Legacy

Martin Luther King Jr. was the voice of a movement that fought successfully against bigotry and suppressive and oppressive laws. He was the voice of timeless principles that reflect humankind at its best, striving for selflessness to achieve justice in the face of hate and violence. He embraced and showed people how to live out difficult paths: civil disobedience and nonviolence. Later in life, he turned his compassion and energy toward fighting poverty and economic injustice, causes that would surely make him less popular but to which he was committed nonetheless.

King's "I Have a Dream" speech today is widely regarded as one of the greatest speeches ever given; in American history, perhaps only the Gettysburg Address rivals it in terms of its influence and reputation. With the speech, Dr. King managed to capture the unspoken and unrealized aspirations of a struggling democracy. "That day," author James Baldwin would write, "for a moment, it almost seemed that we stood on a height, and could see our inheritance; perhaps we could make the kingdom real; perhaps the beloved community would not forever remain the dream one dreamed in agony."

King serves as a reminder of the courage we all have access to when we're fighting for our own rights or the rights of others. In times of turbulence, struggle, or celebration of progress, the spirit of Dr. Martin Luther King Jr. and his commitment to peace and justice is never very far.

It's important to understand and remember that the country's civil rights advances would never have been possible without the brave actions of thousands of individuals. But for so many of these people, Dr. King was their leader, and their voice.

Perhaps the nation's first African American president, Barack Obama, has best characterized the life and legacy of Dr. King:

> *Through words he gave voice to the voiceless. Through deeds he gave courage to the faint of heart. By dint of vision, and determination, and most of all faith in the redeeming power of love, he endured the humiliation of arrest, the loneliness of a prison cell, the constant threats to his life, until he finally inspired a nation to transform itself, and begin to live up to the meaning of its creed.*

CHRONOLOGY

1929 Michael Luther King Jr. is born in Atlanta. "Daddy King" later changes his own name and his son's from Michael to Martin.

1947 King is ordained as a Baptist minister.

1948 Martin Luther King Jr. and Coretta Scott marry in her parents' garden.

1954 King moves to Montgomery to serve as pastor of the Dexter Avenue Baptist Church.

1955 Under King's leadership, African Americans in Montgomery boycott city buses to protest segregation.

1957 Leading Southern clergy form the Southern Christian Leadership Conference to fight for civil rights; they name King as president.

1958 Touring with his book *Stride Toward Freedom*, King narrowly escapes death after being stabbed by an unstable woman.

1959 Martin and Coretta travel to India and learn more about nonviolence.

1960 The sit-in movement begins; King is sentenced to hard time. Presidential nominee John F. Kennedy phones Coretta to express his concern. Hearing of this, blacks turn out to vote for JFK.

1961 Freedom Riders travel through the South. King calms a crowd trapped inside a Montgomery church during a white riot related to the rides.

1963 King writes "Letter from Birmingham Jail." He delivers his "I Have a Dream" speech in Washington. JFK is assassinated. Four girls in Atlanta die in a church bombing.

1964 King is awarded the Nobel Peace Prize. President Lyndon Johnson (LBJ) signs the Civil Rights Act.

1965 King's Selma Campaign takes place. LBJ signs the Voting Rights Act.

1967 King begins the Poor People's Campaign.

1968 King is assassinated on April 4 in Memphis. The nation mourns, and riots break out in cities across the country.

GLOSSARY

Brown v. Board of Education A May 17, 1954, Supreme Court decision that declared school segregation unconstitutional. Written by Chief Justice Earl Warren, the decision stated that "separate educational facilities are inherently unequal."

civil disobedience A refusal to obey laws or commands, particularly those considered unjust, as a means of protest or to seek changes from the government. Often associated with nonviolent resistance.

civil rights Rights guaranteed by the US Constitution and its amendments, such as the right to vote or be treated equally under the law. Derived from the Latin *ius civis*, "rights of a citizen."

Civil Rights Act of 1964 This landmark legislation outlaws discrimination based on race, color, religion, sex, or national origin. It ended segregation under Jim Crow laws in the South.

direct action The use of civil disobedience or nonviolent resistance tactics to achieve specific results. Direct action during the civil rights era included such things as mass demonstrations and lunch counter sit-ins.

Freedom Riders A group of civil rights activists who rode buses through the Deep South in the 1960s to fight segregation. Specifically, they rode to challenge Southern states' refusal to enforce new laws requiring integration of bus terminals and facilities serving interstate passengers.

Henry David Thoreau American writer, philosopher, and abolitionist known for his essay "Civil Disobedience," which argued in favor of resisting unjust governments. The essay influenced Martin Luther King's own ideas about how to bring about racial equality.

Jim Crow A system of segregation in Southern states that strictly segregated black and white races. Based on local and state laws prohibiting integration of schools, libraries, theaters, restaurants, and other public places.

"Letter from Birmingham Jail" Martin Luther King Jr. wrote "Letter from Birmingham Jail" in 1963, after he was arrested for civil disobedience. The letter explains and defends nonviolent resistance to segregation and other forms of racial discrimination and is an indirect challenge to white America to recognize the injustices of the day.

literacy test In the segregated South, states used literacy tests to keep blacks from voting. The tests supposedly determined whether a person could read the ballot, but in fact they were administered with the goal of failing most black test takers. The Voting Rights Act of 1965 outlawed these tests.

Mahatma Gandhi Gandhi led a national campaign of nonviolent resistance that resulted in Britain's withdrawal as India's occupying government. Dr. King was inspired by Gandhi and studied his principles of nonviolent resistance.

Montgomery bus boycott A 381-day campaign during which black citizens of Montgomery, Alabama, refused to ride city buses as a protest against segregation on the buses. After much publicity, it ended with a Supreme Court ruling that segregation on buses was unconstitutional. The boycott helped establish Martin Luther King Jr. as a national civil rights leader.

NAACP The National Association for the Advancement of Colored People is a leading civil rights organization, founded in 1909.

nonviolent resistance Nonviolent resistance calls for the use of peaceful means of protest to fight injustice and bring about social or political change. These means can include sit-ins, marches, and boycotts.

poll tax A fee imposed on people seeking to vote in elections. In the Jim Crow South, poll taxes were used to prevent African Americans from exercising their right to vote. Poll taxes were outlawed by the Voting Rights Act of 1965.

Poor People's Campaign A movement started by Martin Luther King Jr. in the late 1960s to bring about an end to economic injustice and improve the lives of people living in poverty.

Reconstruction The period after the Civil War during which the South was rebuilt and the country was reunited.

segregation The separation of blacks and whites that was set out by local and state laws in the South.

segregationists People who support segregation and may fight efforts to integrate schools or other places.

social gospel A way of living out the Christian faith that emphasizes a commitment to ending social problems such as poverty. The focus of the social gospel is on charity and justice, as well as salvation in the afterlife.

Southern Christian Leadership Conference (SCLC) A network of Southern churches, headed by Dr. King, that led and participated in civil rights campaigns in Selma, Birmingham, and elsewhere.

suffrage The right to vote.

vigilante An ordinary citizen who seeks to enforce laws or social norms–such as segregation–by acting outside the official legal system, often through violence, lynching, or other forms of intimidation.

Voting Rights Act of 1965 This legislation passed under the Johnson administration outlawed literacy tests and other forms of discrimination in voting systems.

FURTHER INFORMATION

Books

King, Martin Luther, Jr. *A Time to Break Silence: The Essential Works of Martin Luther King, Jr., for Students*. Boston: Beacon Press, 2013.

Shetterly, Margot Lee. *Hidden Figures*. New York: HarperCollins, 2016.

Zinn, Howard. *SNCC: The New Abolitionists*. Chicago: Haymarket Books, 2013.

Websites

Freedom's Ring

http://freedomsring.stanford.edu

Listen to Dr. King's "I Have a Dream" speech and compare the speech he gave on the Mall to his written, prepared speech. If you click "Index" (on the bottom left) you'll find a wealth of articles and videos arranged by topics such as "Love and Faith" and "Making Democracy Real."

Gallery of Achievers

http://www.achievement.org/universe

Click around on the planet dots and you may find yourself losing hours learning about amazing people–and their connections to each other. Click on any one person's photo and you'll be linked to a profile of them, photos, videos, and more. Start with Rosa Parks, either by locating her dot or by typing her name in the search bar.

National Civil Rights Museum

http://www.civilrightsmuseum.org/students

Become an investigative reporter in search of a scoop, and you'll experience some of what the 1955–1957 Montgomery bus boycott was like.

PBS: The Rise and Fall of Jim Crow

http://www.pbs.org/wnet/jimcrow/stories.html

Here you can view primary-source documents, see Jim Crow photos, and watch fascinating videos related to life under Jim Crow.

Videos

"Martin Luther King Jr."

https://www.brainpop.com/socialstudies/famoushistoricalfigures/martinlutherkingjr

Brainpop offers a thorough and easy-to-understand video summary of Dr. King's life and work.

"Origins of Jim Crow – Compromise of 1877 and *Plessy v. Ferguson*"

https://www.khanacademy.org/humanities/ap-us-history/period-6/apush-south-after-civil-war/v/jim-crow-pt-4

Learn more about how Jim Crow laws took root in the South and the legal decisions that led to widespread disenfranchisement.

BIBLIOGRAPHY

Branch, Taylor. *The King Years: Historic Moments in the Civil Rights Movement.* New York: Simon & Schuster, 2013.

Carson, Clayborne, ed. *The Autobiography of Martin Luther King, Jr.* New York: Warner Books, 2001.

Colaiaco, James A. *Martin Luther King, Jr.: Apostle of Militant Nonviolence.* New York: St. Martin's Press, 1993.

Hakim, Joy. *A History of Us: Reconstructing America.* New York: Oxford University Press, 2003.

Haskins, Jim. *I Have a Dream: The Life and Words of Martin Luther King, Jr.* Brookfield, CT: Millbrook Press, 1992.

Pollack, Jack H. "Literacy Tests: Southern Style." In *Reporting Civil Rights: American Journalism 1941–1963*, 85–91. New York: The Library of America, 2003.

Smith, Harrison. "What Was Martin Luther King Jr. Like as a Child? A Prankster and 'an Ordinary Kid.'" *Washington Post*, January 15, 2017. https://www.washingtonpost.com/lifestyle/kidspost/what-was-martin-luther-king-jr-like-as-a-child-a-prankster-and-an-ordinary-kid/2017/01/13/391a384c-d853-11e6-9a36-1d296534b31e_story.html.

"The South: Attack on the Conscience." Time.com. Retrieved April 1, 2017. http://time.com/vault/issue/1957-02-18/page/19.

Williams, Juan. *Eyes on the Prize: America's Civil Rights Years, 1954–1965.* New York: Penguin Books, 2013.

INDEX

Page numbers in **boldface** are illustrations. Entries in **boldface** are glossary terms.

ABOUT THE AUTHOR

Jacqueline Conciatore Senter has written for children's publishers, science journals, newspapers, magazines, and in the realm of nonprofit communications. She was a writer and editor at the Jane Goodall Institute for ten years and the National Science Foundation for five. Her hundreds of print and web articles have appeared in numerous publications. She loves American history and lives in Fairfax, Virginia, with her husband, Michael.